*How to Get into Harvard**

*Content in this book is satirical and should not be construed as fact. This book was not produced in conjunction with Harvard College or Harvard University.

Published by Satire V (satirev.org)

ISBN 978-0-578-16635-3

"If you buy only one book teaching you how to become an excellent sheep this year, make it this one!" – Prof. William Deresiewicz

"I wish I'd had this book back when I were in high scool." – Yale Student

"Oh, you're writin' a book? Is it a book called <u>How to Stop Messin' Around and Help Your Dad Mow the Lawn</u>?" – Anonymous Satire V Writer's Father

Also Written by Satire V

Table of Contents

Introduction

Hello, reader!

No doubt you have picked up this book hoping to unlock the secrets of getting accepted to Harvard. We all strive for acceptance. For many, this is living your whole life in someone else's shadow, sacrificing everything with the hope that, one day, you'll be welcomed and appreciated. Putting in 110% until you hear those magical words, "Junior, you did a good job," and tears will stream down your face because you know that papa *does* love you. And he always will. You know that, son.

Much like a distasteful *Hallmark* movie, your journey to Harvard will be filled with predictable plotlines, clichés and forced character development. To help you with your journey, several Harvard students have united to spill the beans on this institution.

This book covers many of the premier strategies on obtaining that acceptance letter as well as many lesser-known tactics. So sit back, relax and enjoy the ride – or that's what we *would* say if this process wasn't going to break you. You should really get that heart rate up.

Good luck! You're going to be completely reliant on it.

1

Testing Positive

Harvard University prides itself on minimizing the importance of test scores. Standardized testing, a 20th century phenomenon that is in its infancy when compared to this institution of nearly four centuries, fails to reflect the full scope of a student's knowledge while placing arbitrary barriers to their success in the form of "test anxiety."

❋ ❋ ❋

One numerical rating system for students, Grade Point Average (GPA), comes with a preponderance of flaws. A high 4.0 GPA could reflect academic achievement, but it could also be the result of a student taking and breezing through a class like Quantum Hydrodynamics for which they are greatly overqualified. Similarly, a low GPA of 4.0 might be the result of bad teachers or exigent circumstances rather than a student's lack of effort or understanding. The Harvard admissions office recognizes results produced by standardized testing and the GPA system are hardly accurate enough to give them a central role in admissions decisions. As a result, test scores and GPA results, so long as they are perfect, will play next to no role in the admissions process.

Despite this assurance, an overview of the GPA statistics for a typical incoming class might be of use to some prospective students. Of the 2,047 students admitted to the class of 2017, roughly one hundred percent had an unweighted GPA between 4.0 and 4.0. Taking various systems for measuring honors credit into account, the range shifts to between 5.0 and π^π!. The median unweighted GPA was 4.0, with a standard deviation of 0. The mean GPA of an incoming freshman is approximately 4.0, and the mode is 4.0. Of course, these figures are merely guidelines, rather than a recipe for admission to Harvard. Students are judged holistically, and some very well-rounded and talented students have been admitted with GPA's as low as 4.0. The ultimate message here is to not let your GPA be an impediment to your choosing to apply to Harvard. Whether your GPA is 4.0, 4.0, or just 4.0, you certainly have a shot of admission to Harvard University.

While it cannot be emphasized enough that your perfect test scores, just like your perfect GPA, will not be a huge factor in your admissions decision, it's impossible to submit a perfect standardized test score if you haven't taken any standardized tests. In the sections that follow, we will be discussing a number of different options from which to choose.

The Tests

Now that we've discussed Harvard's philosophy on test scores, it's time to start taking some tests. Between your 8 AP classes, charity work, astrophysical research, and the commitments of running a Fortune 500 corporation, it might be necessary to make some tough decisions in order to fit standardized testing into your busy schedule. When it comes to college entrance exams, you've got two main options: the ACT and the SAT. When choosing between the two there are a lot of factors to consider. Additionally, like all binary choices—whether liberal vs. conservative, boxers vs. briefs, or Kirk vs. Picard—there is a right answer. It is our intention to put all the facts on the table, and it is your job, as an aspiring Harvard student, to read our minds and figure out which test we subtly hate for no reason.

Before getting into the substance of each test, it seems valuable to compare the backgrounds of the two. The SAT, which stands for truth, justice, and the American way, is a three-section test covering the three "r'"s: reading, riting, and rithmatic. What do you mean they got rid of writing? Shut up. The SAT's governing body, an organization whose name is unpronounceable in the human tongue but is sometimes referred to as the College Board, is based in New York City near the campus of Columbia University, the greatest of the lesser Ivies. The ACT, which apparently doesn't stand for anything anymore, is a test composed of five sections: Reading, Science Reasoning, Mathematics, Writing, and Counting. The test is administered by ACT, Inc., which is based in Iowa City, Iowa, a city that is sometimes referred to as the New Haven of the Midwest.

3

The ACT, otherwise known as the Yale of college admissions tests, is sometimes chosen by aspiring college students because it is slightly easier. In recent years, the number of students taking the ACT has grown dramatically, and in 2011 the ACT exceeded the SAT in total participants with 1.66 million, approximately 99.96% of whom did not get accepted to Harvard. Early in the ACT's history, the Science Reasoning portion was accused of "heretical witchcraft," both for implying that maggots do not spontaneously arise from rotting meat and for being notoriously difficult to master. In order to placate the science section's detractors, a new section of the test, Counting, was added in 2009. Students will be given between four and eight small objects and asked to indicate the number of objects to the test proctor by a show of fingers. Extra credit is awarded for completing the section without attempting to eat the objects in question.

The SAT, a test renowned the world over for its objectivity and accurate measurement of human intelligence, has historically taken a more central role in the college admissions process than the ACT. The test, administered in a clean-room environment by trained psychologists, is divided into 10 sub-sections, 3 in each of the subjects and a 10th called the "experimental" sub-section. The experimental section, used to probe the darkest mysteries of the human mind, can appear to be a sub-section from any of the three subjects, but on closer inspection it is much more than that. Questions that have been included in past experimental sections include math: "What is the difference between a duck", writing: "Identify the single error in the following sentence: 'Has anyone really been far even as decided to use even want go to do look more like?'" and reading: "You're in a desert, walking along in the sand, when all of a sudden you look down and see a tortoise, Leon. It's crawling toward you. You reach down and you flip the tortoise over on its back, Leon. The tortoise lays on its back, its belly baking in the hot sun, beating its legs trying to turn itself over, but it can't. Not without your help. But you're not helping. Why is that, Leon?" The experimental section, just like the other sections, brings out the worst in you, but that is what college is all about.

SAT	ACT
· Scores out of 1600 or 2400 · Offered seven times per year · Provides a way of demonstrating fealty to our Reptilian overlords · Success on test correlated with overall evolutionary and reproductive fitness	· Scores out of 36 · Offered only during eclipses · Angers the Reptilians and hastens the demise of our world · Success on test indicates only that your parents don't love you enough to pay for SAT tutors

So, you've gotten a 4.0 GPA and perfect scores on the ACT and SAT, but so what? With Harvard's holistic acceptance system, it's not enough to just ace a couple tests and hope to get in; you have to ace dozens of them. To aid you in this goal, we've compiled a helpful list of the best tests for prospective Harvard students to take.

Table 6.1—AP Tests:

A crucial part of the New World Order, the AP tests function as a way for our benevolent leaders at the College Board to sculpt our educations outside the confines of the SAT.

AP US History: A passing score on this test is not expected or required by the University, but answering the question about the year of Harvard's founding wrong will eliminate you from consideration.

AP Latin: Lorem ipsum dolor sit amet, consectetur adipisicing elit, sed do eiusmod tempor incididunt ut labore et dolore magna aliqua.

AP Physics B: Instituted as a replacement for Physics A, which was phased out after current Physics Department Chair Melissa Franklin scored an unprecedented "6".

AP Studio Art: 3D Design: Often called the easiest AP test, folding the exam booklet into a cube grants a score of "5."

AP Music Theory: An experimental exam designed to test how well students perform on a test for which no course is taught.

THANKS/APOLOGIES TO M. C. ESCHER AND CAMILLE FLAMMARION

There are also other standardized tests you can take!

Table 6.2—Other Standardized Tests

PSAT: Ever wanted to take the SAT and then divide your score by ten? If so, you're in luck. For Harvard applicants, the PSAT is merely a formality necessary to receive your National Merit Finalist award.

PLAN: Cleverly avoiding litigation replacing the PSAT's "divide by 10" model with a patented "subtract 4" system, the PLAN offers students the opportunity to take the ACT twice without gaining anything from the experience.

IB Tests: See *How to Get into Yale*

SAT II Subject Tests: After proposals for a 23-section SAT test were struck down by the 5th Circuit Court for violating the 8th Amendment to the US Constitution, the College Board instead instituted the SAT Subject Tests in order to satisfy their home world's demand for innocent blood.
·   Mathematics Level 2: Much like the Math section of the standard SAT but without all those pesky shapes. Harvard admissions policy requires a score of exactly 783.
·   Biology E/M: Despite what you may have read in Liberty University's prospective student materials, the Biology subject test has an "evolutionary biology" version paired with its microbiological version. Students may elect to take either version at test time, but Ken Ham is always watching. As is God.

Foreign Examinations: For non-Americans without access to the greatest primary education system in southern North America, proving your academic credentials can be tough. Harvard grudgingly accepts a number of SAT/ACT alternatives.

Table 6.3—Strange Foreign Exams

OWL: Administered to all 16-year-old British students, the OWLs test a variety of skills crucial to success in elite UK institutions like Oxford and Cambridge. Harvard attempts to maintain the same standards as the Oxbridge schools when evaluating the OWLs, but tends to put less emphasis on the coherency of one's Patronus.

CLEP: Also administered by the College Board, the CLEP has the notable downside of actually being a venereal disease. Students should be advised that Harvard will consider credits from the "Business" exams valid if and only if they are first submitted to MIT and then forwarded to Harvard via a system of subterranean pneumatic tubes.

GKISPE: The Glorious Kim Il-Sung Presidential Examination, seen worldwide as the pre-eminent college entrance exam, is the only test whose results can be submitted in lieu of a standard application. Covering subjects as diverse as the diet of the unicorns that once roamed the fields of Pyongyang and the first words spoken by our Eternal President Kim Il-Sung upon his miraculous birth atop the All Seeing Peak, the GKISPE is the most comprehensive test of world knowledge known to man. Achieving a perfect score is only possible if you have welcomed Juche into your heart, but cutting the great Western Demon out of your life is the only way to know the peace of the Glorious Democratic People's Republic of Korea.

2

Correspondences

A lot of letters are exchanged in the course of the college application process. The following are examples of letters taken from this process.

❋ ❋ ❋

Dear Prospective Student,

Greetings! My name is Hubert G. Collins, Director of Admissions and Financial Aid at Harvard College. I've received many letters over the years from people asking me about the Harvard admissions process, and so I figured that instead of responding to each of you individually, I'd write down everything in one letter and send it to every publisher that I can think of. That's a lot of publishers, and our Admissions Office intern poisoned himself from licking the backs of too many stamps. Therefore, if you're reading this, it means that someone chose to publish my letter, and that the death of our beloved intern Brian Hamilton was not in vain. Brian, we will keep your memory in our hearts forever

Additionally, I have included a selection of letters that the Admissions Office has collected from students' mailboxes and dorm rooms when no one was looking. I hope you find it edifying in your college application process, and at the very least I hope that you find it entertaining. The cards and writings have been carefully curated to provide an interesting and thought-provoking piece. Ideally, they should read like an epistolary novel. If you don't know what "epistolary" means, then you probably won't be admitted, unless you're a legacy, in which case: welcome to Harvard!

In general, however, I highly recommend that you do not send the Admissions Office any letters. I repeat, do not write to us. Do not ask us questions because the chances are that we are asking ourselves the very same questions. "But how will I know which parts of my extracurricular work to highlight in my applications?" you may ask. "My classical saxophone virtuosity? My charity organization that takes underprivileged children to the zoo? My other charity organization that helps animals break out of the zoo to avoid abusive zookeepers by placing them discretely in the backpacks of said underprivileged children?"

The truth is: we don't know, but if I had to sum up our admissions process in one word, I'd say that it is *holistic*. This means that we look at the whole student. We usually start at the toes, and work our way up from there. If there's something we don't approve of, then we chuck the application into the "Rejections" bin. With the remaining applications, we create two equally-sized piles, and then we leave it up to Associate Director of Admissions Charles A. Tanner to make the final decision.

Charles A. Tanner is a half-blind cat that we found wandering around the Harvard Square MBTA station very late one evening, but we could tell that he had a knack for this sort of thing. Whichever pile he chooses is accepted into the College, and the pile he does not choose is either rejected or goes into the Wait List, a purgatory filled with nightmares, tears, and disconnected phone calls from high school advisors.

Dr. Tanner employs a very sophisticated method to determine which students he admits, and it would be pointless to attempt to describe it for you. In fact, he has never described it to us either, and he tends to be fairly laconic, apart from the occasional growl or hiss. Therefore, it is impossible for me to explain to you the exact details of the complicated method that Dr. Tanner no doubt employs in his decision-making. I can assure you, however, that he has never regretted any admissions decision he has made, and neither do we. Furthermore, because Dr. Tanner has never revealed his exact age to us, we can only assume that he brings hundreds of years of experience to what is always a very difficult process.

With that, I invite you to peruse the following selection from the Office of Admission and Financial Aid's archives of letters and correspondences, and I cannot wait to read all of your applications this coming fall!

Warm regards,

Hubert G. Collins

Director of Admissions and Financial Aid, Harvard College

Part II: A Letter to the Soul

Editor's note: The following are excerpts from the diary of Brian Hamilton, our beloved, deceased intern. Although technically they are not letters, they refer to a series of letters that were particularly important for the Admissions Office, and they are also addressed as "Dear Diary", implying that Brian's personal reflections were intended as a correspondence with the diary.

Dear Diary,

Here we are, another noontide at the Admissions Office. I am at my post in the back corner, where they have commanded me to sit, twiddling my thumbs. They told me specifically to twiddle my thumbs.

I can see the mailman walking up to the building. It's almost time for me to start sorting and delivering the letters to the admissions officers. Sometimes it's just too painful to think of all those people across the country—nay, the world—who write here, hoping against hope for some escape to the humdrum of high school ennui, the rarest piece of advice from a sage of Harvard admissions who has a key to their salvation—or their damnation…

Every day, I wake up and thank the heavens that I got into Harvard. I love it here.

Love as always,
Brian Hamilton

--

Dear Diary,

I got a letter! I shall copy it to you in its entirety:

Dear Mr. Hamilton,

Howdy! My name is Francine LeCompte, and I'm currently a high school student who's applying to Harvard. I had a couple of questions about the admissions process, and I was wondering if you might be able to answer them.

First, can you let me in? Ha ha! I'm just kidding. (That was a joke, in case you didn't notice. Amongst my many passions, I'm an aspiring comedienne, and I founded my high school's Comedians for Immigration Reform club. We perform immigration-themed skits and stand-up at local bars, community centers, and preschools. I thought you might want to know that.)

My main question is about the application essay question. As it is now, it seems a little vague: "You may wish to include an additional essay if you feel the college application forms do not provide sufficient opportunity to convey important information about yourself or your accomplishments." To tell you the truth, I found the rest of the college application too restrictive, and I have so much to say about myself that I'm afraid I'll exceed the word limit. Instead, I think it would be much more amenable for both of us to chat on the phone or in person. I can fly into Boston for a day or the next four years—either one! (Another joke!)

Yours truly,
Francine LeCompte
Lincoln, Nebraska

GPA: 4.7
"She's an excellent student, with a passion for chemistry and history, a gun, and an ebullient personality."—Fred Grayson, Principal

Admittedly, she meant to write to Associate Director Harold Hamilton. Nevertheless, I shall treasure this scrap of paper as a serendipitous message from the universe. Who knows on what magical path I shall be led by similar occurrences of chance, happenstances of the Fates? I shall also compose another letter informing young Francine that she had the wrong address.

As always, I shall write to you again. Do not fret, my silent companion!
Brian Hamilton

--

Dear Diary,

Young Francine seems to have misunderstood my earlier missive. She has responded to me, flirtatiously, it seems, mistaking my interest in her ability to contact Associate Director Harold Hamilton with some other motive. I imagine she shall attempt to use her wiles to seduce me into revealing the secrets of the Admissions Office. But I shall not! I am as an obelisk in the Egyptian desert: no matter how buffeted by the sandy winds of the world, I shall not collapse into decrepitude, but shall stand tall. I shall be faithful to the Admissions Office.

I will promptly respond to young Francine to notify her of her grave error.

Until the morrow, tome of my soul!
Brian Hamilton

--

Dear Diary,

My steadfastness and fortitude have served me well, for this morn Director Hubert G. Collins himself endowed me with a task in accordance with my talents. Indeed, whereas formerly I was merely the passive recipient of the mail, now I shall be entrusted with the *sending out* of correspondences. Indeed, this is truly an impressive accomplishment. I shall promptly add it to my résumé.

As to the saga of young Francine LeCompte, I am afraid that my previous attempt to dissuade her from the path of untoward licentiousness has gone unheeded. On the contrary, she somehow discovered my phone number (on the nefarious Internet, I presume) and has been heckling me with inane "texts" and "Snapchats." The latter is merely a stream of harmless and silly images presented in a temporary, ephemeral fashion: Francine holding a gun in front of a river, Francine holding a gun in front of a tree, Francine holding a gun in front of my house (how blithe childhood seems these days)! Nonetheless, these annoyances are filling my proverbial inbox, and I am, as they say, miffed.

Until next time, my sweet, silent guardian of thoughts and ruminations!
Brian Hamilton
--
Dear Diary,

Young Francine has appeared at the Admissions Office, wielding a gun and several blunt objects picked up from the environs of Harvard Square (including a fence post and an 18th-century gravestone), demanding to know the secrets of Harvard admissions. But do not fret! Sound of mind and trained in Jujitsu, I waylaid her with a well-timed and impeccably executed roundhouse kick.

I am afraid that we shall not be hearing from young Francine for several years, although I doubt that her arrest will have much bearing on the Admissions Committee's decision for her application (we have accepted much worse in the past, trust me). And, as reward for my valor, Director Hubert G. Collins himself endowed me with a sticker and a mission. Indeed, now I am entrusted with the task of ensuring the delivery of the Director's own correspondence with local publishing houses. He seeks to enlighten the public as to the processes of the Admissions Office, without (I hope) revealing too many of our most cherished secrets.

Away I go to lick the stamps of these missives.

Parchment of my spirit, I shall write to you soon!
Brian Hamilton

15

Part I: A Familial Correspondence

Dear Franklin, my darling son,

I can't tell you how proud I am of you for deciding to apply to Harvard. Mostly, that's because I don't like to rank my children as somehow "better" or "worse" than each other. But if I had to decide, I'd now definitely put you above your brother Jack and somewhere below your sister Madeline. That's how proud I am of you.

If you get in, you might even top Madeline! How cool would that be?

It definitely takes a lot of guts to even apply to Harvard. And not just normal guts--metaphorical guts, too. We're talking grit, moxie, spunk, backbone, fortitude, mettle, pluck: all of these words mean "guts," and I found them in the thesaurus that I bought for you today. I've heard that high-quality synonyms are the key to an outstanding application essay, so don't forget to check the thesaurus for every single word. Remember: no matter what you write, it's not sufficiently suasive until you supplant all of the scribbles that you scrawled. That's an important piece of motherly wisdom, and I've provided you with some ink and a needle so that you can tattoo it on your arm.

I know what you're going to say: "That's all great, Mom, but how am I going to concentrate enough at home to write my application when everything is so noisy, between Madeline reading her books and Jack playing alone in the dungeon?" It's true—sometimes our house does get kind of rowdy. Thankfully, our dungeon is pretty insulated from the noise, so I kicked Jack out and set up a little office for you to work in!

As you can probably tell, the dungeon is now much cleaner now and includes a computer, a printer, several notebooks, and the complete works of Vladimir Nabokov. Technically, the door is locked from the outside, but you can just knock and I can come and let you out.

16

Lots of love,
Elizabeth (your mother)

--

Dear Mom,

Thanks. Can you let me out?

Love,
Franklin

--

Dear Franklin,

Thank you for passing the first draft of your application under the door. I've tried to fit some crackers through that opening so that you can eat, but they didn't fit, so I ate them.

By the way, I don't want you to think that I'm punishing you by keeping you in the dungeon because you wrote a mediocre essay (we'll get to that later). On the contrary, I lost the key. But don't worry, your father and I are looking for it! I would never punish you like this.

But back to your essay. To be honest, I was a little confused about what exactly you were trying to say. "Dear Mom"—what does that mean? Why are you talking to the admissions officer as if they were your mother? I'm your mother! Next, I do think that it's important that you thank Harvard for considering your application, but it's probably not right to do that in the essay. Similarly, it's creepy if you tell them that you love them.

I did, however, like the bit where you wrote, "Can you let me out?" It was very interesting in a minimalist sort of way, like an existential cry for help shouted into the blizzard of society. I'd like to see some more of that.

Keep trying,
Elizabeth (your mom)

FROM: frank_the_tank21@hotmail.com
TO: charles.tanner@admissions.harvard.edu

Dear Dr. Tanner,

Hi! My name is Franklin [redacted], and I'm a prospective student from [redacted], Indiana. I'm really excited to be applying to Harvard, and I can't wait to send you my application. My parents are also really happy that I decided to apply, and my mother has been particularly supportive.

Actually, that's why I'm writing to you. I think my mother is a little worried about the application, and her nervousness is affecting me.

Actually, that's putting it lightly. I'm scared, Dr. Tanner. I'm scared and alone.

Anyway, if you could maybe let me know how to reassure her that everything's going to be okay, it would be a huge help to me. I figured you've probably seen situations like this in the past, so maybe you have some advice? Maybe a brochure or something?

Thanks so much for your help. I'll see you in the fall (please)!

Best,
Franklin [redacted]

FROM: charles.tanner@admissions.harvard.edu
TO: frank_the_tank21@hotmail.com

Dear Sir or Madam:

I will be out of the office. I'm not sure when I'm coming back, but I'll probably be back eventually. If you really need to contact me, don't.

Best,

Dr. Charles A. Tanner
Associate Director of Admissions
Harvard College

Dear Franklin,

I haven't been at home recently, and I'm sorry that you haven't gotten anything to eat recently, but really you shouldn't be distracting yourself with things like food and water. Do you think all the other kids you're competing against need to eat?

Incidentally, this is the second day I've been in the hospital. Last Sunday, I was walking home from water aerobics when I was attacked by a feral cat.

By the way, your brother Jack came to visit the other day, which I quite appreciated. Unfortunately, that means I'm going to have to rank him above you. And don't even get me started about Madeline. She's so far beyond both of you that you'd need a telescope to see how high I rank her.

Sincerely,
Elizabeth (your mom)

3

What is a Legacy and Why Do I Want One?

If you find yourself asking the question, "What is a legacy?" it means that you don't have a legacy, you will never have a legacy, and your chances of getting into Harvard are about as slim as a white girl's chances in a drinking game against a sewage drain.

❋ ❋ ❋

Now, if you find yourself asking the question, "Ok. Well then, why am I reading this section, or even this book?" then you're smart, and you might just have a shot of getting in, but still probably not. This chapter will tell you exactly how to do that by giving you the keys to unlocking the most elusive door of the admissions process: legacy.

In today's world, the most common use of the word "legacy" comes from the world of sports: athletes like LeBron James and Ray Lewis always talk of their hunger to win championships and solidify their legacy among the greats of their games. But the whole point of legacy at Harvard is to steer clear of today's world: you can't build your legacy on your accomplishments or even the accomplishments of a team that includes you. In fact, you shouldn't even *try* to accomplish anything when attempting to create a legacy; you'd just be wasting your time. Rather, you have to steal directly from the accomplishments of others.

What you must come to understand is that legacy at Harvard is about an arbitrary connection to the past. It's about something that's old, that shouldn't matter anymore, that doesn't matter anymore, but somehow carries the most weight in your application. Namely, it's about your parents.

Did your father go to Harvard? Yes? Then you have a legacy. Did your mother also go to Harvard? Yes? Then you have a double legacy. TRICK QUESTION! Your mother went to Radcliffe. We're going to have to work on this. But that comes later.

Basically, for now, what you need to know is that in addition to rewarding your seven successful campaigns for school club officer positions, in addition to rewarding your 56.84 GPA, and in addition to rewarding the ridiculous amount of effort and stress that led to your fantastic SAT score, Harvard rewards you simply for the womb you came out of and whoever came into it. And, unlike the rest of the stuff you put on your application, legacy is a criterion that is completely determined at conception—much like life itself (you're going to have to learn to take a conservative stance on many issues if you want to be a legacy. So get used to it).

This makes legacy probably the most difficult criterion on a Harvard application to achieve. Now, you may be thinking, "Wait. So I start out from birth with an inherent disadvantage? That's, like, the stupidest thing anyone's probably ever heard."

But don't fret, reader. We here at Satire V would like to help you even the odds. The following sections will include tips and tricks that can make even you a legacy.

Table 9.1—Steps to Successfully Becoming a Legacy

Step 1: Forge documents

If you're going to become a legacy, you're going to have to learn a lot about the government. After all, Government will be your major. TRICK QUESTION AGAIN! It's called a *concentration*. If you don't remember that, no one will believe your father (not your "dad") went to Harvard.

The best way to get a head start on your government studies is getting to know some personal government documents. Specifically, birth certificates, driving records, criminal records, or anything with your name on it.

And, with a few pen strokes, you can take common last names and make yourself the benefactor of a Harvard legacy fortune (one that hopefully made Harvard a benefactor of its fortune). Here are some good examples as rough guidelines:

1. Lamar"ont"
2. Green"ough"
3. Elliot (use only one "l" like in "Elitist")
4. Zuckerman"berg"
5. Strauson
6. Wigglesworthstein
7. Clarkson Pforzheimer

If you don't know why these names are significant, you probably shouldn't even go to college anyway.

Names to avoid: Kaczynski and Howie Mandel (Not that he has anything to do with Harvard; our focus groups show that people just don't like that name).

Step 2: Ask everyone what House they were in, no matter what or when or why

Legacy kids know that when their relatives see or meet anyone else from Harvard, the first question out of their mouths is, "What House were you in?" You have to copy this, and then some.

First, start with Harvard students and alumni. When you see anyone wearing salmon-colored shorts, immediately run up to them and say, "Nice shorts. Speaking of shorts, what House were you in?" When you see anyone playing spike-ball, grab the ball, put it in your pocket, extend your hand for an introduction to each player, and ask "What houses were you in?" When you hear anyone use the terms "quantitative" or "qualitative," turn to them and say "Qualitatively, what House were you in?"

To get some practice, you don't have to limit yourself to just Harvard students and alumni. If you're in the grocery line and the cashier asks you "Credit or debit?" say, "Cabot...My mom was in Cabot...What House were you in?" When you get on a plane and the cockpit's door is still slightly open, lean in and cordially say to the pilots, "You know what they say: time really 'flies.' Haha. Remember those college days? By the way, what houses were you two in?" See a homeless person on the street? Go approach them and ask, "What house ..."

Actually, don't do that one.

Step 3: Get a lot of money

If you are a legacy, then your parents went to Harvard. If your parents went to Harvard, then they got nice jobs. If your parents got nice jobs, then you are loaded.

That proof is called a *reductio ad absurdum* (it's not actually that, but the more Latin logic terms you know, the more legacy you have, so memorize it!). So it's true. And if it's true, then it's Veritas (more Latin! See?!). You need to make sure you have some cold hard cash by the time you apply. Here are a few ways to do just that:

1. Open a lemonade stand
2. Open a lemonade stand
3. Open a lemonade stand
4. Open a lemonade stand
5. Strip

IN CASE OF EMERGENCY ONLY: Step 4: Get adopted

If Steps 1-3 don't work (for instance, if you're the child of a Soviet-era spy and thus have no government documents, and you have a strange inability to ask questions, and you have no business acumen whatsoever), you can always try the patented emergency Satire V Tremendous Other Plan (STOP): get adopted.

This is probably the most difficult step listed here. But it's also the most permanent and secure.

By using the cleverness of a Harvard student who could probably get in without legacy, you can get adopted by a legacy family, thus legitimately giving you actual(ish) legacy. Here's how:

[Editor's note: the Satire V author of this section was a legacy student. As such, he does not have the "cleverness of a Harvard student who could probably get in without legacy" and was unable to finish this section. We apologize for the inconvenience. We would have fired him, but his parents paid for this book to get published. That's just the way the world works, I guess]

So you're a legacy. Now what?

You did it. You're a legacy student. Congratulations. That's really great. Or, in more legacy terms, really nifty, or really swell.

But now comes the tricky part—what are you going to do with it? Some choose to ignore it. Others don't hide from it but still choose not to willingly bring it up. And a brave few travel to the Hamptons every weekend with their hired ghostwriter to get away from the pressures of their mid-town Manhattan high-rise, living the lifestyle that the country's founders intended legacy students to have (yeah, they all went to Harvard too).

So here's a profile of the two most common ways to go about living out a Harvard legacy:

Legacy shame:

This route is taken mostly by kids who still think the world is somewhat fair and that they can make a difference in it, even though their only struggle in life has been justifying the fairness of their matriculation to Harvard as a legacy student and their only accomplishment in life has been getting into Harvard (partly because of their legacy status).

Of course, you earned your own legacy, and these people did not. And that lack of earned accomplishment drives their insecurities to a point where they won't talk about their legacy at any cost. If you ask them what school their parents went to, they'll say, "Boston." When you reply, saying that wasn't an answer to your question, they'll say "Boston." And when you point out that their second response didn't make any sense at all in the context of your conversation, they'll take off sprinting the other way, maybe in the direction of Boston. But most likely not.

Legacy pride:

This is the completely opposite path. It embraces legacy and milks it for all it's worth. And it takes no shame in doing so.

These students often take pride not in their own accomplishments, but rather in those of their ancestors, who came to America only with some pocket change, a glimmer of hope, and a team of servants that fit into their personal cabin on a European colonial ship in the 19th century. Since their ancestors struggled for their success, many of these legacy students are perfectly fine with the lack of struggle for their own place in the world, redefining "struggle" as having only one country home on Martha's Vineyard.

But even this legacy lifestyle has its pressures: final clubs measure the true worth of any of these legacy students entering Harvard's doors. As John F. Kennedy once said, "If the young men and women who are fortunate enough to enter the prestigious doors of Harvard University do not gain entrance to one of its final clubs, they are pussies." In short, legacy kids who do not become part of a final club are not worth their weight in their parents' gold.

So, ladies and gentlemen, that's it. Satire V has shown you the importance of legacy, how to become a legacy student, and what to do with a legacy. Now it's up to you.

Just remember, when it comes to legacy, you're either born with it or you're not. But no matter what, you can always become a legacy, with a little hard work. Otherwise, the application process would be a meaningless and archaic mess, selecting candidates with an arbitrariness that's unfit for the leading schools of our nation.

But it's definitely not that. Definitely.

4

Elitists Come in All Shapes and Sizes

Harvard has recently received far too much praise for its attention to diversity. While it is true that this class is the most diverse, that doesn't mean its diversity is interesting. The class of 2019 has got some pretty boring backgrounds. But word on the street is that this year that's all about to change. If you're looking for a golden admissions ticket (which, side-note, would be an awesome way to deliver acceptance decisions, because chocolate) then you need to be in tip-top diversity shape.

❋ ❋ ❋

Here's a little secret: Harvard actively seeks out part-mythical or alien students. After all, it's magic and alien technology that allows the endowment to double every six years. But Harvard likes to switch it up from time to time. Critics have been raving over what this season's new look will be. Last year it was Pygmy Jawa, but this year correspondents are saying colleges are looking for something a little more outrageous! And while we don't know for sure, our team of researchers has a few predictions about what this year's look *won't* be.

Table 2.1—What Harvard Doesn't Want
1. First of all, after the whole Elizabeth Warren ancestry scandal, Native Martian is out. Tough luck, kids. It's not that schools don't like the alien look, but no one will believe you now if you say you're Cheroglee, S-iouxx, Naavaajo, or Bopi. Native Venusians are still welcome, though; it's too interesting to pass up.

2. Second, like, if you're part-Bigfoot, that's fine and like, you can still apply and stuff. But you should at the very least try to be Chupacabra, too. Our staff thinks that goat-sucker is the new black. There are so few at Harvard, and so this new stuff is thrilling to a lot in admissions.

3. Next, still no Time Lords. We don't know why.

4. And finally, something Harvard does want: if you have any history of airbending, earthbending, waterbending, or firebending, the admissions office will eat that shit up.

Satire V's Guide to Making Your Story Suck Less

When it comes to your race, you *must* be original. Get some gumption, be creative, and make anything up. But don't fall for the Na'vi trap; you just won't be able to fake a 10-foot tall blue humanoid as well as you can fake the others. If there's one thing Harvard is known for, it's taking its Pandoran population seriously.

If you absolutely *must* use your original race, then find a way to manipulate it. Mention the word nomad; it's a sure thing. And always remember that key word: persecution, persecution, persecution.

Regarding your belief system, chances are good you'll be rejected if you don't choose a new religion by the age of 16 and have a big blowout with your parents; get to it.

DISCLAIMER!!!

With all these tips and pieces of advice, it's easy to see how crazy some devoted candidates can get when they decide to apply to Harvard. It goes without saying that Harvard is indeed an incredibly diverse school, and based on these predictions, it's only becoming more diverse, something the student body treasures and encourages. But with diversity comes a price. And we would be remiss not to warn you about what that price could be.

When forced to live among others different from yourself, you will be confronted with many challenges. What, for example, will you do when your roommate is of a different color or creed? Of course it's possible the two of you could become best friends and go on movie dates all the time or something. But it's also possible she could kill you in your sleep. Is that a risk you're willing to take? The point is, we don't know her or where she comes from, and she could be dangerous.

Being among people that are different from you can be emotionally challenging as in other ways. Sometimes, while the other girls braid their hair and you can't, you might feel lonely or excluded. Seeing people pray in public could be uncomfortable for you, and the different shades of skin could just be too much sensory information for your eyes to handle. Or at least that's what my grandpa always says.

Sure, this might be a great opportunity for you to be the first one from your village to attend college, but in the end, it's pretty unwise, because what if you feel scared? What happens if you get really nervous and shaky? What about when you're tired or don't want to do your homework because it's boring? Our official advice? Diversity can be scary.

Putting it All Together

Remember, even if you're not one of the things mentioned above, there are still ways to jazz up your story! The following are a few examples of successful diverse applications:

Table 2.2—Awesome Stories

Leila Reem: Leila is from Saudi Arabia. Unfortunately, everyone and their mother are from Saudi Arabia these days. But Leila also has a secret that Harvard admissions thinks is pretty cool. Leila's dog is gay. And in a place like Saudi Arabia, this kind of life of secrecy is a far cry from easy. Her story, one of grappling with loving her dog for who she is, coming to understand her role as an ally, all while dealing with her dog's incessant shedding, is a new one. Admissions called her story "edgy" and "sophisticated" and "umami." Leila's heartbreakingly nuanced video diatribe to the admissions office, which includes a personal breakdown next to her dog, is certainly umami. That's why she got in.

Luther Zimbabwe: I want to be clear with you in saying that this particular success story's real name is not Zimbabwe. Rather, it was his first strategy employed to get into Harvard. It became a real nice tearjerker when he wrote that "for years I'd identified as a Zimbabwe, but never been given the chance to be who I was due to my spiteful Republican parents." In reality, Luther's life story is bleak. A California native with lots of leadership experience from National Honor Society, Luther decided to apply to Harvard as a senior, knowing that he'd need some way to make himself seem interesting. He threw away the Axe and the Hamburger Helper, trading it in for a life of... well, the same, but now his last name was Zimbabwe and the admissions office thought that was really cool.

Randall Spitz: Randall comes from a wealthy family, but he's also half-cheetah. This is what we call a 'shoe-in.'

5

How to (Physically) Get Into Harvard

Okay. The easy part is over. You've filled out your application, written a great essay about saving some orphans from illiteracy (and maybe actually saved said orphans), forged the perfect letters of recommendation, and congratulations, you've been accepted to Harvard! Or not. Doesn't really matter. Either way, your greatest challenge is yet to come, actually getting into Harvard.

❋ ❋ ❋

Although it may not get as much attention as Harvard's low acceptance rate, the task of infiltrating Harvard's campus has crushed the dreams of just as many over-achieving try-hards as the Admissions Office. Before you can pass through Harvard's ivy-covered gates as a graduate, you must first scale said gates in the dead of night or uh, walk through them during the day, I guess. Even locating Harvard within the Dadaist-planned city of Cambridge has defeated more than a few National Merit Scholars (well over a dozen if you include Semi-Finalists, but since when do they count?). As documents obtained through the Freedom of Information Act have now revealed, President George W. Bush's infiltration of the business school campus was a key factor in his father's appointment as Director of the CIA and was later used as a blueprint for CIA operations in Central America and the former Union of Soviet Socialist Republics. Likewise, U.S. Senator Ted Kennedy himself only found his way to the safety of a Harvard dorm room after being sewn into the lining of Bobby's futon and smuggled through Harvard's picturesque Johnston Gate.

If you hope to join the ranks of Harvard's prestigious alumni then, like them, you'll have to find a way inside the walls of Harvard Yard. The path to the smug superiority of a Harvard graduate is fraught with danger. Panhandlers, signature-seeking activists, under-paid security guards, and slow-moving packs of tourists will all stand in your way. Further, to truly experience all Harvard has to offer, you'll have to infiltrate more than just the Yard. Pseudo-secret all male societies, overly pretentious and sub-par humor magazines, fraternities that want to be final clubs, and Lamont Library are all central to the Harvard experience and entrance to each poses its own unique challenges.

Getting into Harvard isn't easy. It requires *years* of hard work and dedication or *years* of being related to someone else who worked really hard to get in. Regardless, if you're willing to put in the work, this chapter will give you all you need to know to get into the world's most prestigious university as well as our best tips for penetrating the shadowy recesses of Harvard nightlife.

"Enter to Grow in Wisdom"

As you have probably heard, Harvard is almost impossible to get into but even harder to get kicked out of once you're in. In fact, just getting into Harvard Yard is likely to be the most challenging part of your Harvard experience. Once you're inside the pee-scented brick walls of Harvard Yard and standing next to the famous pee-scented statue of John Harvard, everything else will just fall into place.

Though by far the most obvious entrances to Harvard, make no mistake, entering through one of Harvard Yard's many gates still requires careful planning. A foolish mistake like confusing the Class of 1887 Gate with the Class of 1877 Gate could bury your dreams of a Harvard degree beneath a pile of non-lethally armed campus security officers.

However, with the proper preparation and tactical guidance, it is entirely possible to just walk into Harvard Yard like it's some kind of privately-held-but-open-to-the-public college campus. To that end, here are several tried-and-true methods for infiltrating Harvard Yard:

Table 3.1—Methods of Infiltration
1. *"The Tourist"* – Harvard Yard is visited by literally a million tourists every day [citation needed]. Fortunately, these hordes of academia-obsessed visitors provide an excellent source of cover for entering Harvard Yard unnoticed. Simply position yourself in the middle of a moving crowd of tourists and pretend to be enthralled with Harvard's Georgian architecture. For added realism, be sure to suddenly stop moving every few seconds to photograph one of the dozens of empty chairs occupying the Yard.

2. *"The Tour Guide"* – Similar to above but with some slight changes. Wear some sort of Harvard apparel and shout "facts" about Harvard's campus while walking backwards with total disregard for your safety and the safety of those around you. Within a few minutes, you should have gathered at least a dozen prospective students and overbearing parents who will dote on your every word and follow you like some sort of pied-piper of prestigious degrees.

3. *"The Sophomore"* – This strategy requires slightly more preparation but has a much greater potential pay-off. Walk around with a backpack and if challenged, claim to be a sophomore from Leverett House concentrating in Economics. By my estimation, roughly 65% of Harvard undergrads are sophomore Economics concentrators from Leverett, so you should blend right in. This strategy will let you walk right in to not just the Yard, but hyper-secure areas like the Science Center and historic Sander's Theater, where famous textbook author and amateur philatelist N. Gregory Mankiw is rumored to have been spotted by my freshman roommate.

4. *"The Diplomat"* – Our most complicated strategy also has the highest potential pay-off. You will need to rent at least two large, black SUVs and hire a number of large, intimidating-looking men (bonus points if they are visibly armed). Bribing a police escort is helpful, but not entirely necessary. Sit in the backseat of one of the SUVs and instruct your newly-hired security detail to drive in formation and approach one of Harvard Yard's main gates. Confidence is key here, as you'll have to pass yourself off as some sort of foreign dignitary. I'll leave your exact identity up to your discretion, but it is vital that you appear unreasonably annoyed at being even approached by security. If possible, take time to remark on the relative youth, and therefore, inferiority, of Harvard when compared to the Universities in your home country.

5. *"The Steam Tunnel Repair(wo)man"* – Our last method for getting through the gates of Harvard Yard actually involves circumventing them entirely. Beneath the surface of Cambridge lies a vast network of steam tunnels. Originally planned to serve as a rapid-transit system for Harvard's elite after they shed their physical bodies like the husks of ripened grain, these tunnels now serve primarily as a clandestine meeting place for Harvard Republicans to discuss their feelings and share erotic poetry about Ayn Rand. Fortunately, they also provide a convenient means of covertly entering Harvard Yard and/or getting those pesky wrinkles out of your robes – I mean clothes. We wear clothes here... perfectly ordinary clothes. Throw on an orange vest and hardhat and enter the tunnels through one of the many steam vents outside Harvard Yard and follow it to its source beneath historic Harvard Hall, the hub of Harvard's hot-air circulatory system.

I Love the Nightlife, the Nightlife Has Mixed Feelings about Me

So you've gotten into Harvard (or not) and, thanks to my brilliant and easy-to-use tactics and maneuvers, you've actually gotten onto campus. For many, this is where they would stop; content to rest upon the laurels of their over-priced education, but not you. Mt. Auburn St cries out to you with the siren song of a hundred girls in impractical footwear. Who are you to resist its call?

All over Harvard's campus (well, not the Quad, but almost all over), parties are being thrown by final clubs named after stupid and/or imaginary animals, fraternities full of people that couldn't get into a final club, and literary societies that are way too hip to associate with the first two groups but still kind of like Natty Ice. Accessing the inner sanctum of Harvard's nightlife as a freshman won't be easy (unless you're a girl or a man with androgynous features) but it is possible. By utilizing one or several of the following methods, you'll be drinking shitty keg beer and wondering why the floor is so sticky in no time:

Table 3.2—Nightlife Access Points

"The I-Am-an-Attractive-Woman-That-You-Would-Like-to-Sleep-With" – This one more or less explains itself.

*

"The One-of-the-Girls" – If you can't be one of the dozens of girls in tight dresses being ushered into final club basements, the next best thing is to be ushered in along with them. Simply find a pack of attractive young women heading to a final club or party, the larger the better, and follow them from a safe distance. When they arrive at their destination, quickly close the distance between you and them and attempt to blend in as part of their group. Roughly 45% of the time, you will be completely ignored and allowed to slip inside with your considerably more appealing companions. The rest of the time, you will be embarrassingly singled out and asked to leave. A man's game charges a man's price.

*

"The Wall-Jumper" – You may have noticed that many final clubs have walled backyards where they host numerous parties. You may have also noticed that Harvard Campus Services have a tendency to leave ladders just lying around…

*

"The Celebrity" – Do you look like a celebrity? Can you convince a drunk person that you are that celebrity? If the answer to either of these questions is maybe, it's probably worth a shot. This tactic is especially effective for gaining entry to parties held by humor magazines that still desperately cling to a reputation for producing famous comedians and actors roughly 30 years after such a person was last a member. BJ Novak was really funny in that one episode of the Office, though.

*

"The I-Am-a-Member-of-this-Private-Club" – This strategy is not recommended as it typically requires 6 months to a year of putting up with abusive, vaguely-homoerotic bullshit followed by years of paying absurd amounts of money, but if you happen to be ludicrously wealthy or a varsity athlete, you might want to consider actually joining a final club, in which case you will usually be allowed into their parties.

Parting Thoughts

With the above methods, you now have all you need to know to both get into Harvard and to make the most of your time in Cambridge, except for math, but that's what concentrating in Government is for.

Congratulations and welcome to Harvard! You should also probably read the rest of this book.

6

How to Make Sure Others Don't Get Into Harvard

This chapter is objectively the most important in this entire book. The rest of How to Get Into Harvard gives you innumerable hints, tips, nips, and quabs on how to get into Harvard, but this is the only section in the book that'll drop the deets on how to foil your nemesis.

Destroying all semblances of competition is a crucial part of your journey to the bum-piss gilded streets of Cambridge, Massachusetts. NEWS FLASH: More likely than not, only one person from your high school, or even your town, is getting into Harvard. Even if you do happen to go to a school that generally sends more than one student to Harvard a year, there is surely someone who you don't want ruining your college experience by being present.

For example, when this author was a young girl, her nemesis and was an equally beautiful, intelligent and special boy named Zane Wheelbrock. But this author knew something that others did not. Zane was an annoying prissy little copycat. How dare you try join National Honor Society, Zane? When you knew I was trying to join National Honor Society. Who the did you think you were?

Anyway, listen up, kids: admissions officers are not infallible (the primary reason that the Authors of this Book are currently Harvard students), so as a rule, someone's got to make sure all the terrible people you know don't even stand a chance. So suck it, Zane W. Suck it hard. I hope you're enjoying your forced gap years in Siberia.

At this point, you make be asking, "But why should I take it upon myself to permanently alter someone's course in life.

"I AM NOT GOD!" you sob.

Woah, first of all, take it down a notch, bro. You're right; you are not God, but that is no reason to soil the pages of this book with your disgusting mortal tears.

Pick yourself up off of the Home Depot showroom floor and realize that there are plenty of reasons that you are good enough to make these decisions for other people. Here's a sampling of some of those:

1. You taught Elvis Presley pretty much everything he knew.
2. Despite being slow-witted, you already have a scholarship to play football at the University of Alabama.
3. You're a decorated Vietnam vet.
4. You've founded and run a hugely successful shrimp company
5. You're the captain of your cross-country team.

I could go on and on about how great you are. I could even direct an Academy Award winning film based on your awesome life. As you watched it, all 142 minutes of it, you'd realize that you are more than qualified to decide whether or not the friends, family, enemies and strangers in your vicinity can accompany you to Harvard, or if they must perish for four years in the bowels of New Haven, CT at the school we have all come to know and loathe – Southern Connecticut State University.

QUIZ: Is your nemesis worth sabotaging?

Before you continue on with the rest of this chapter, you need to take a good, long, hard look at your situation and decide if it's really worth intervention.

1. Smell them. What does he or she smell like?
    a. The pained, never-ending tears of the innocent and Axe Body Spray

     b. "Trying too Hard," a scent by Stepdads Going Through Midlife Crises

     c. Incriminating files at a medical malpractice firm

2. What do they normally eat at lunch?

     a. Shredded Beef salad, no dressing – the midday meal of champions. Warm, grizzly, chewy meat over wilting lettuce. This shows strength, character and a hardened, patriotic American spirit.

     b. Fish Pies—this person displays his or her bold character by eating fish in the middle of the day, but let's be real, who eats carbs anymore? And let's pretend gluten isn't poison.

     c. 1 Stack OfficeMax® Copy Paper – your nemesis noisily eats another leaflet, staring you down with robotic green eyes.

3. Who does your mother like better?

     a. Your nemesis!

     b. You!

     c. To have "one fucking second of peace and quiet around this goddamn house, goddammit!"

4. Can they beat you in a footrace?

     a. Absolutely—Sucks to suck, bro.

     b. Absolutely not – Wow, do you want a fucking cookie?

     c. No legs. -- N/A (unless they write a tear-jerking essay about it)

5. What is the last thing you saw him or her reading?

     a. A Choose Your Own Adventure Novel about Karate – Reading is for simpletons and the weak of mind, but a CYOA novel is an exceedingly classy choice, symbolically representing the reader's ability to impose his or her will on the author.

     b. The Harvard Crimson -- It's official. This person cannot read. But he or she does understand the importance of always looking as if you at some point have learned to read.

     c. *How to Get Into Harvard*

MOSTLY As-- High threat level -- Holy SHIT, this person is a champion. Skip all the pansy stuff and default to "Shooting the Dog". Yes, I am recommending that you <u>KILL THIS PERSON'S DOG</u> THE DAY BEFORE THE INTERVIEW. It is that serious. This person will either steal your spot at Harvard or even worse: accompany you to Harvard.

MOSTLY Bs -- Basic threat level—don't worry too much about this guy. His or her chances are pretty mediocre, and they'll probably ruin it for themselves anyway.

MOSTLY Cs – This person is very obviously not going to Harvard, and is probably a paper shredder.

The Plots

Now that you've figured out exactly how much energy you should put into destroying your nemesis, it's time to choose their poison(s).

Table 10.1—The Interview Plots
1. The Dog F. Kennel-dy:

Execution: Take ol' Rex out back the night before the interview.* There will be lots of tears the following morning and the mental stability of your nemesis will be called into question.

You'll Need: A gun (or a knife if you're feeling a little stabby and/or you don't pass the gun license screenings), and to be a firm believer in the fact that *All Dogs Go to Heaven* (1989). Except for that one that totally goes to hell. One dog goes to hell.

*If they don't own a dog, buy them one and murder it.

43

2.   The Coitus Interviewus:

Execution: Walk in on the interview and start having a conversation about your achievements. Who says three's a crowd?! If anyone tries to steer the conversation back to your nemesis, simply open your mouth wider, and speak with increasing volume until your nemesis shuts up about whatever non-profit they pretended to work for last summer.

You'll Need: Brazen confidence and that special twinkle in your eye that makes everyone at the table wonder if they're going to be murdered in their sleep

Table 10.2—Standardized Testing Plots

1.   The Lickitung

Execution: Score a seat behind your nemesis and get really close to licking the back of his or her neck, but never actually make contact. He or she will feel real creeped out the whole test, but not really know why! Guaranteed to bring a ~2300 caliber score to the low 2000s!

You'll need: A tongue so long and moist that it can cause paralysis, a number two pencil, and an eraser.

2.   The ACT

Execution: Convince your nemesis to take the ACT, the SAT's kind-of-slow distant cousin.

You'll need: A nemesis who doesn't understand acronyms.

Table 10.3—Application Plots

1. The Common App Switcheroo

Execution: Log into their common-app account and replace all the text with all the One Direction erotica you can buy.

You'll Need: Your nemesis's common app login info, OR the ability to pull off a Hollywood hacking montage (bonus points if you're one of those NEC dual-degree bastards and can compose the background music yourself). You'll probably also need a Club Penguin membership.

2. The Nation Builder

Execution: Fly out to the impoverished country your nemesis has done service work in and, using everything you've learned from AP Economics (you got a 3, right?), raise the GDP to at the very least $1,700 billion. Once you've done this, all the work that your nemesis has done there will be completely invalidated because people who take service trips to first-world countries are just glorified sex tourists.

You'll Need: The spirit of a true American, and the Extreme Home Makeover team.

7

"Should I Apply to Harvard?"

We have already spent time telling you how to get into Harvard, but you still may be asking yourself, "Do I really want to apply to Harvard? Is it really all that great?" While we would certainly like to respond to your question with a confident "Yes" preceded by a slap to your face for asking such a stupid question, it's only right we help you to make an informed decision. Below, you'll find a totally unbiased account of each of the Ivy League schools, based on firsthand imagined experience.

Penn

After leaving the armored bus that takes you into the heart of Philadelphia, you find yourself in a large concrete compound with walls that extend into a haze of barbed wire, broken glass, and 10,000-volt wires. You are quickly handed the requisite identification so that the authorities will be able to identify your body: papers, visa, student ID, salmon shorts. A passed-out freshman is carried by on a stretcher held by two frightened-looking dentistry school students. Passing through Locust Walk, you are accosted by Wharton School students howling against the bars of their cages, clambering for the Adderall that your tour guide has given you to placate them. And then you lose your tour guide, only to find him three days later taking a nap in a kiddie pool of jungle juice.

Dartmouth

I remember my first college visit was to Dartmouth. My grandfather and twelve of his vertically-challenged yet horizontally-gifted friends scooped me up from my humble home and led me through the wilds of New Hampshire to Dartmouth, or The Lonely Mountain, as we called it. Unfortunately, the college was less than spectacular. It supposedly sported well-equipped facilities in the mid-1800s, but the faculty delved too greedily and too deep. Isolated in the mountains with no one but the small student body, the rapacious few awoke a great evil. Do you know what Dartmouth's school motto is? *Vox clamantis in deserto*. Do you know what that means? "The voice of one crying in the wilderness." Crying in the fucking wilderness. 2/5, would not matriculate again.

Columbia

I had personally never been to New York City before and didn't know what a long flight it would be. The campus is beautiful once you get there, I never realized how mountainous and tropical Central Park is. My host, Juan Carlos, was incredibly friendly and introduced me to all of his "compadres," as Columbia students call each other. Student groups are incredibly active and even go on weekend excursions, or "trafficking treks," regularly. Juan Carlos introduced me to everyone in the Spanish club, *Las Fuerzas Armadas Revolucionarias de Colombia*, who were all bursting with energy as we did some volunteer work transporting something called *cocaína*, which, as far as I can tell, is a type of laundry detergent that people sell as part of their work-study arrangement. I didn't get to see much of the dorm rooms; Juan said there were too many *yanquí imperialistas* around.

Cornell

I was so excited to fly back to New York City (I think I landed in the Bronx, because it seemed pretty far from Columbia), see the big city lights, the hustle and bustle of Times Square, and then get on a dilapidated Greyhound for what felt like ten years. But as the third driver told me (the other two mysteriously disappeared while driving in the middle of the highway), it's the journey that counts. Driving through upstate New York, you learn a lot of things about the Erie Canal, but you also learn a lot of things about yourself. For instance, I learned that I am considered "muggable" by the great majority of people who go on Greyhound buses. Also, I learned that I am very talented at getting old gum unstuck from the sides of windows. Perhaps most importantly, I learned that each person contains a spark of beauty within them. This is especially the case if that person smokes on a bus, and a bump in the road causes them to inhale several burning pieces of tobacco. Let me tell you, I have some epic stories from this trip. None from Ithaca though, which sucked by the way.

Princeton

Located in Princeton, New Jersey; a fine township sometimes referred to as "the valley of ashes." Sure, the orange and black school colors may be easily mistaken for the uniforms of the college's neighboring prisons, but once you realize that every single person on campus is a white billionaire, you realize that, since you're not on Wall Street, you must be at Princeton. If you have a tan or a Mazda, Princeton may not be the place for you. That's not to say that Princeton discriminates. Old money, new money, what's the difference? Aren't we all the same in the eyes of the tuition collection agency?

Yale

Now before I say anything, I know you're just going to think "ooh Harvard-Yale, total rivalry. There's no way this guy is going to give a fair assessment." Now that's untrue. My brother actually goes to Yale (he's slightly shorter than me) and I've visited him many times (each resulting, mysteriously, in a case of bronchitis). From what I've seen of Yale's campus, it's actually pretty up to par. The library is the third largest academic library in the country and is located just 134 miles south of Cambridge, Massachusetts, home to the *largest* academic library in the country. The faculty is second to one. But the food is really fantastic. It's just perceptibly worse than Harvard's—not a significant amount, but just enough to notice. My little brother—well, I *call* him my little brother—he's older but Grandma always says hello to me first. Anyway, he really likes it there, so I guess there's that.

Harvard

Each morn he wakes to the babbling of the Charles, the lark in his window chirps that it's time to break fast, and as he slips from his silk-sheeted mattress, the servant, Winston, robes him in the requisite Ermine (Tuesday is fur-shawl day), this young man oft finds himself thinking back to the immortal words of American philosopher, author, philanthropist, and talk-show host Oprah Winfrey: "Oh my goodness! I'm at *Haaaaaaarvard*![1]"

After a delicate melody on the joys of life, sung whilst woodland creatures assist in preparing the morning meal, it's off to class where he learns about public-domain texts from tweed-donned professors (whose British accents rival those of the most famed Oxford dons). Even the trees are made of brick in this crimson paradise. After some quick work on groundbreaking research, it's off to dinner where Scarlett Johannson awaits wearing one of those weird single piece nipple-banana hammock bikinis like the one from Borat, except it's totally hot because she's not Borat. It's then off to the squash court for a quick workout before reading e. e. cummings's original notes as a preparation for the sweet dreams of sleep, which can be no better than life awake. Our dear student disrobes himself of the ermine and rests his weary, genius head after another magical odyssey of a day.

---

[1] Winfrey, Oprah. *Harvard Commencement Speech*. May 31, 2013.

EDIT: Stanford

My editor sent back the original draft of these summaries, telling me I forgot to include all of the Ivies. It seriously took me four hours on Collegeboard and Wikipedia before I found out that Stanford counts as an Ivy League school. So maybe I'm not in the happiest mood about writing another review, but if WILLIAM is going to make me write another, I guess I have to. Fine. Okay, let's see. First off, California? Established 1891? That makes less sense for an Ivy than a motto that isn't in Latin, i.e., *Die Luft der Freiheit weht*. That's German, people. Not the most beautiful language in the book. What's it mean anyway? Quick Google translate.... Aannnd... "The wind of freedom... blows"? Fuck you Stanford, the wind of freedom doesn't blow. The wind of freedom rocks, the wind of freedom kicks ass. If it weren't for the wind of freedom and my grandpappy, you all would be speaking German right n---oh I get it.

EDIT 2

Shit. Okay. Well it looks like Stanford *isn't* an Ivy, but I should have been writing about some place called ***Brown***.

Table 8.1—So, Should I Apply to Harvard?
1.   Does your father, like King Laius, the father of Oedipus, want to leave you to your death on a windswept crag? Go to Cornell.
2.   Are you grandma's second-favorite? Go to Yale.
3.   In a hole in the ground there lives you? Go on an adventure! To Dartmouth!
4.   Fleeing the Puritans from threat of the stocks? Go found Brown.

5. Have you no sense of decency, sir? At long last, have you left no sense of decency? Go to Penn.

6. Does your father drive a Mazda? Do not go to Princeton.

7. Still think you look good in that jean skirt? Go to Brown.

8. Hmmm, this one seems to be a total loser. HUFFLEPUFF!

9. ¿Quieres ganar some real fuckin dinero? Vete a Columbia.

10. Do you own the Tuesday requisite ermine? Go to Harvard.

11. Wenn ist das Nunstück git und Slotermeyer? Ja! Beiherhund das Oder die Flipperwaldt gersput!

12. Would you like to beat on, as a boat against the current, borne back ceaselessly into the past? Go to Princeton.

13. Do you look stately in the Tuesday requisite ermine? Go to Harvard.

14. Are you a go-getter, following the voice of your heart as it leads you onward into that adventure we call life? Then don't let me tell you what to do! You be you!

15. Is the voice of your heart still talking to you? That may be a problem.

16. Do you want to spend ten years trying to get back home for break? Sneak into Cornell inside a wooden horse.

17. Love America? Go to Stanford and teach them a lesson in freedom.

18. Scarlett Johansson? Very nice, how much?

19. Do i carry your heart with me (do i carry it in my heart)? Go to Harvard.

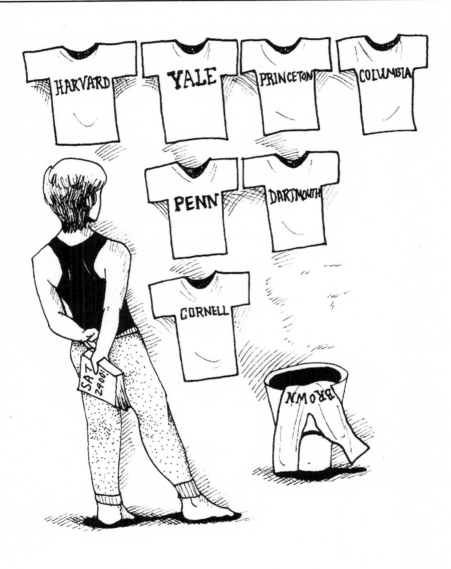

8

Writing the Perfect College Essay Perfectly

Now you're probably in a semi-state of panic because you have no idea what a college essay is and how to go about producing one. You're in a maze of fear, doubt, and probably questioning everything you know, like whether that talking pizza roll in your head is real or not (it is). Well luckily you called me, and I'm here to solve all your problems. I am an experienced college essay writer and I've helped many students get into college.

❋ ❋ ❋

It's easy! You just pick whatever college you want and walk into one of the buildings. There! You're in college, thanks for reading and send a check for $1,000 to the Trump Hotel and Casino in Atlantic City, New Jersey, care of Herman Plancker. I'm gonna hit it big soon, you guys, I just need a little more money.

Oh. They're telling me I actually have to tell you how to write an essay on getting into college. Well, put the pizza rolls into the oven and check on the hookers in your basement because it's going to be a long night and I've already done that.

To begin, you need to understand what the essay means. Colleges don't actually care about the essay, it's just a way for them to see that you're not an illiterate moron. Or a real person and not a Filipino child trying to scam financial aid out of the system. YOU GIVE ME BACK MY FIVE GRAND YOU LITTLE RASCALS!

First, the essay is a chance for you to distinguish yourself. If you *aren't* an illiterate moron, this is your chance to prove it. Second, the essay can hurt you if you don't do it right. If you write your essay on the bottomless chasm that is your ex-wife's soul and how she destroyed your life, then admissions officers aren't going to look too favorably on you.

The essay is a story and most good stories are told in a classic three act structure. Anything else is either pretentious or just stupid. There should be an introduction, setting up the situation and what you're going to write about. The body should explain the situation, and tell the reader how you acted and why that was different from anyone else. You should have examples that illustrate your personality and do everything you can not to be seen as mentally deficient. These examples should be specific: any one moron can write down that they were a part of a card counting team in Las Vegas, but only someone who's actually done it can describe the hatred and fear on their teammates' faces when I ratted them out to casino security in exchange for immunity. The final part, otherwise called the conclusion, is where you bring all your ideas and examples back together into one place (like a basement) and tell your reader why you're the most qualified candidate for their institution of higher learning.

Finally: proofread. In the vein of not wanting to look like a moron, make sure you spell all your words rihgt and make sure your punctuation is where it needs, to be. Also, make sure you don't get pizza sauce on your essay. That stuff stains, you know. Have one of the hookers in your basement read your essay, too, because they might see things in it that you missed or wouldn't have thought of otherwise.

Anyway those are the basic guidelines for writing your essay. Follow them and you can have a bulletproof essay in no time.

55

Inspiration

Without a doubt the single most important element of any essay is the inspiration behind the words, the backstory that forms the foundation of your future literary masterpiece.

To make things a little easier, here is an inspiring story from another student:

Table 7.1—Inspirational Stories
One young man grew up a long time ago in a desert far, far away from Harvard. To protect his identity, all names have been omitted. He had a single mother who did the best she could to raise him, but at the tender age of 9, he started working in an auto-body shop. He was a precocious youngster and pretty soon knew his way around all the machines in the shop. On the side, the boy started racing as a hobby and got pretty good at it, hitting the underground circuits to win his family some money so they could escape the grasp of his tyrannical boss. This continued until a foreign traveller arrived one day. The traveller recognized the boy's talent and helped free him from his boss. Upon leaving with the traveller,

he was instantly caught up in a giant war where he helped destroy an enemy base. After that, he joined an ancient order dedicated to the protection of the galaxy and eventually became Darth Vader. Now that's something you can put on an application.

Anyway, the point of the story is to write an essay that's engaging and will hold the readers attention. Unfortunately, the boy in the story above, whose name I still won't say, came off as flat, boring, one dimensional, whiny, and ultimately kind of a jerk. He didn't get into Harvard, and he later lost his Sith internship.

Conclusion

William Shakesman once said, "To thine own self, be true." WELL THAT'S A LOAD OF CRAP! Writing your essay should be about the farthest thing from the truth as you can imagine. You need to come off as smart, sophisticated, worldly, wise beyond your years, and totally incapable of committing a multiple homicide.

In a way, an essay is kind of like a court case: if they can't find any evidence to convict you, they let you go. The same concept holds true for essays. If they can't find a reason to put you in a dumpster, then they move you on to the next part of the process. Ultimately, an essay can't really help you but it can hurt you, so use the tips in this chapter to write the best essay you can!

9

Extracurricularious!

So here's the tricky part: Extra-Curricular Activities. People may tell you this is the fun and exciting part where you get to try new things— that's not true. This part is scary. Whatever you do, do not take risks. Extra-Curriculars are what can really make or break your application. For instance, my friend Susan had great grades, a great SAT score, and excellent teacher recommendation letters. But she still didn't get into Harvard. Why? Lack of extra-curricular activities. She only had twelve. She had to take a crack year. Not a gap year. A year smoking crack. It looked great on her resume though. She goes to Harvard now.

✽ ✽ ✽

You know the saying "don't judge a book by its cover?" The college admissions version of that is: "Judge every student very harshly by their extra-curricular activities and make sure they are president of every club or reject them." It's often chanted to the tune of "Imperial March" from Star Wars.

Harvard especially looks for students who are well-rounded, which of course refers to belly size. Admissions officers really like fat kids. Overweight students are the precious gems who dare to swim against the current of society, the ones who aren't afraid to be themselves.

For all you fit and healthy people, this chapter is especially important, so drop your goddamn celery sticks and bright purple shake weights and listen up. This section is critical. This section is the end all be all of "things you must know." Like it. Love it. GOTTA HAVE IT. This section is where your application can really shine, like the forehead of a middle schooler going through puberty.

Extracurricularious!

Firstly, take a moment to note the difference between Extracurricular Activities and Extra-curricular Activities. It is vital that you recognize this.

"Oh I know!" you exclaim. "This is like what we do in my AP English class! The dash connotes that you're doing additional 'curricular' activities, whereas the one sans dash refers to activities that aren't academic. It's like in *Much Ado About Nothing*, when Beatrice says--"

No, you're wrong. The difference is that one has a dash and the other doesn't. It's like Golding's *Lord of the Flies:* no symbolism, no allegory, no nonsense. They're just some kids that got stranded on an island. Refreshing, straightforward literature.

In the spirit of *Lord of the Flies*, don't overthink your extra-curricular activities. It's really simple – so simple, in fact, that we've broken it down into twenty-three and a half steps, with some of the harder steps broken down into phases, and some of the phases then split into steps*. Take note not to confuse 'steps' with 'steps*.' And no, the asterisk does not connote anything. Don't overthink it. Or do, and get lost in a web of lies you'll never understand.

***There are two different approaches to choosing extra-
curricular activities:***

---

(1) Go all-in on one extracurricular.

For instance, let's say you have an interest in politics. Most students will
be content with interning for a Congresswoman, or campaigning for the
NRA, or signing petitions in support of the new dog park tax; to get into
Harvard, you must do all of these *and more.* You need to petition the
zoning board to allow the construction of new condos in the river valley.
Then you have to advocate in favor of the new dam that will flood the
river valley. Then you'll lead a multi-million dollar lawsuit against the
construction company that built the dam to compensate the condo owners

for their flooded homes. Pretty soon you won't just be a blatantly hypocritical activist: you'll be a Harvard student.

(2) Have a huge spread of extracurriculars to illustrate the diversity of your interests and passions.

You don't want to hole yourself into one thing, so this is where you take on *everything*.

Remember that you have to be the president of every organization you're in, and sometimes even just being the "president" isn't good enough. Come up with more powerful and fierce titles to really set you apart from the other applicants, like "Czar of the Poetry Club," "Emperor of the Knitting Club," or "Dictator of Model United Nations."

Selling It

So what good is a club you started to raise money to fight Ebola or working for a nonprofit if you don't get credit for it? That's why you have to *sell it*. Here are some tips to use on your college application so that no good deed goes unnoticed.

Tip #1: Here's a tool to help you make a bland extracurricular sound more exciting. Use Old School English words to describe them.

Table 1.1—Old School English to Impress	
Groke	To gaze at somebody while they're eating in hope that they'll give you some of their food
Ballaster	One who supplies ships with ballast
Wamblecropt	To be overcome with indigestion
Bezonter	An expletive denoting surprise
Zemni	A blind mole rat
Snollygoster	A dishonest or corrupt politician
Gongoozle	To stare idly at a canal or watercourse
Dormedory	A sleepy, dumb person who does not get on with work

Mazzebah	Ancient Jewish sacred stone pillar
Callipygous	Having shapely, beautiful buttocks
Slapping	Very good, or fast
Snudge	To stride like you're super busy when you're really not

Sample Paragraph:

I want to become a doctor because I would always groke and then eat but then become wamblecropt! It seemed manageable at first but then bezonter! I became lazy like a snollygoster who gongoozled instead of working. I didn't want to be a dormedory so I took a class on medicine—a real one, not a hoax—and it turns out I am slapping at it! That's what inspired me to work instead of just snudge!

Tip #2: Cool fonts. Cool fonts are essential to any good description.

LUNCH MONITOR

Lunch monitor

Lunch Monitor

Lunch Monitor

Lunch Monitor

·-··.·· --· · · -·. · · · · ·----- · · - ---- · -·

Sample Sentence:

·· want to become a **DOCTOR** because ·· would always groke and then eat but then become wamblecropt!

Wow! Look how we spiced up our sample sentence. If that doesn't get you in, the admissions officer is probably a zemni (in which case, try brail).

Tip #3: Adding "if you know what I mean" after a description.

Example: I'm passionate about burgers! After working hard and trying to figure out what I wanted to do in school, I became president of the In-N-Out Club, if you know what I mean.

Extracurricularious!

Tip #4 Comprehend how to utilize voluminous etymons

Available online at Amazon and at your local Barnes & Noble, given one is still standing.

Tip #5 When describing your extracurricular activities, always sum up your description with "in conclusion..." This will make it very clear that your last sentence is the last sentence.

Example: In conclusion, serving as president of my school's vice-president's club proved to be an extraordinary experience.

Pro-tip: In conclusion, if you are worried that you're taking on too much, you're on the right path. Getting into college is all about being as stressed as possible, if you know what I mean! Feel free to tell your friends as frequently as you like about how much work you have, and how tired you are, and how stressed you are. They'll eat it up!

10

Not Having Money: The Chapter

Harvard University, as you probably know, is the richest university in the galaxy, with billions on billions in the bank. The university has a well-earned reputation for giving generous financial aid. In fact, their current policy states:

"If a w'rthy und'rgraduate joins ye olde college and hath not the surname Boylston, Kennedy, Goldman Sachs, Gates, Rockefell'r, Obama, Cl'rox, 'r Jesus, he shall passeth through with nay fee."

❋ ❋ ❋

Approximately 57% of current Harvard undergraduates fall under this generous policy, the highest ever since its inception at the dawn of time in 1636. But, if you're right at that awkward level of wealth – like your mom bought you a car in high school, but you're 89% sure that a cat gave birth in the backseat; you still rinse and reuse plastic cups at home; or you could pay for your senior trip, but had to ride in the luggage bay of the Peter Pan bus to get there – you will soon find that you will need more money than old John H hands out.

Life in Cambridge ain't cheap, baby. When your trillionaire roommates peer pressure you into drinking some molten gold on a particularly memorable Saturday night, you'll wish you had some spending cash to pay for an ambulance from Thayer Hall to Health

Services. Yeah, yeah, of course you could work as a research assistant for your teaching fellow with the strange wheeze, or even take up a more honest job like cleaning athletic facility bathrooms or stealing positions from unionized locals. But let's face it – those jobs are sweaty and boring, old sport. And you didn't just shit literal gold to be sweaty and boring.

So that leads us to an investigation of the more unconventional "scholarship method." You've probably seen many students claiming success from this path, but to be honest with you, I'm starting to think it's all an elaborate scam. Check out this "award-winning" letter I found online last week:

"DEAR SIR OR MADAME FINANCE OFFICER

Hello! I am PRINCE Dmimba Jackal, and I send My Greetings from Namos (THIS IS THE CAPITAL OF MY BEAUTIFUL COUNTRY OF JUMULA)!! I am writing with WONDERFUL news, as there has been an admission of me to an ILLUSTRIOUS institute – HARVARD university in CAMBRIDGE, Massec., USA.

But there is A PROBLEM!! MY FATHER, the KING of Jumula, has gone MISSING! :((((Our Royal Forces are searching but have found nO SIGN of him. This is very, very BAD FOR ME. I do not have access to the ROYAL FUNDS as I am but a humble prince but I WISH TO ATTEND this ILLUSTRIOUS institute.

I have heard that your organization provides FUNDING for people to ATTEND ILLUSTRIOUS institutes. I am writing for this FUNDING. Please wire, AS SOON AS POSSIBLE, to my bank here in Lagos (account number #3920493910393r092394092, under the name "HAILE ROFESA") the amount of 29 million USD AS THIS IS THE TUITION OF HARVARD. Thank you. I and my country will repay you in FULL PLUS 45% INTEREST WITHIN ONE MONTH OF RECEIPT.

Please pray for my father's safe return I will see the money soon thank you,

PRINCE DMIMBA JACKAL"

I don't know – it just looks sketchy to me. The royalty, the caps lock, all of it. I found another letter, equally suspicious:

"Dear Dr. Jackson,

I wanted to take a moment to thank you for the excellent work that your foundation does for those in need. Even if I do not end up becoming a recipient of the scholarship, I very much appreciate the mission of the Learning Together Foundation, and its commitment to educational access.

Attached is my application to the fund; I have worked hard on it, and hope that my work is pleasing to you. Please let me know if you have any questions about the enclosed materials. Thanks again for the opportunity.

Sincerely,

Oleg Mandelstein"

I don't buy the genuine appreciation, nor the name "Oleg Mandelstein." So, I've decided based on this sampling that all scholarships are frauds. Kids, if you're looking for money, hooking and drug dealing seem to me to be the only reliable options. I could give you the name of a few great cartels.

Based on this belief, I'm not quite sure why you people tapped me to write this introduction, but what the hell? Enjoy your conspiracy. I'm out.

Now What?

So you've made it this far and still want to apply for a scholarship. Good for you, kiddo. Here's a list of various scholarships available for various students from various parts of the world, perhaps one will apply to you:

Table 4.1—Scholarship Associations that Definitely Exist

Chain Smoker's Fund – Are you that kid that smokes 3 packs a day and hangs out behind the auditorium, even on weekends, talking to kids considerably younger than you and generally coming off as a skeezy creep? What's that? I can't hear you over your coughing. Yes? Great! Here's a scholarship for you because no one else cares about you kids. If you can't run one lap around the track without wheezing uncontrollably and hacking up blood, you automatically qualify.

*

Honorable Southern Gentleman Scholarship – This fund is bequeathed on behalf of Beauregarde Atticus Landry, a fine Son of the Confederacy who supported the education of young, white males seeking status in Southern Society. You have to have been born below the Mason-Dixon with a penis and a fine Southern accent, and also sign a document saying that if you become governor, you'll never, EVER let the Yankees take down that Stainless Banner from the top of the State House, so help you God.

*

PornHub Scholarship – This scholarship is paid for by the accidental traffic you give to our obnoxious pop-ups when you select one of our fine videos and by a tariff on the bank account information that those ads ultimately steal. So, logically, we have enough money to send you to the fucking moon, build a Martian university, staff it with professors, and pay for you to go there. If you can just find and hit the "APPLY" button on our well-organized website, the money is yours. Just as long as you stay away from that RedTube horseshit.

*

NeoNazi Trust – This fund is bequeathed on behalf of Beauregarde Atticus Landry Jr., a fine Son of the Confederacy who supported the education of young, white males seeking status in Southern Society. You have to have been born below the Mason-Dixon with a sturdy, white penis and a fine Southern accent, and also sign a document saying that if you become Governor, you'll never, EVER let the Yankees take down that Stainless Banner from the top of the State House, so help you God.

*

Survivors of Future Disasters – Are you a straight up, stone cold G? Smoke crack in playgrounds? Shit on tombstones for fun? Keep hydrated with acid rain? Sounds like you're a old-fashioned, low-quality human being, which means you're like the human version of the cockroach: you're statistically more likely to survive a future apocalyptic disaster and repopulate our planet with your seed. If that's the case, we might as well put you through college first.

*

The Forty-Niners Scholarship – Helps young persons in their pursuit of an M.R.S. degree (or, alternatively, an M.R. degree. We're cool like that). Paying only for sorority fees, Colgate Tooth Whitener Strips, and implants, this scholarship may not cover all incidental costs during your time in college, but it will at least get the important parts. With this very important head start, you should be able to obtain the rest of it after a few consecutive weekends hanging out in a hotel lobby bar or your favorite Final Club basement. If the recipient does not successfully procure a degree (READ: ring) at the end of the four year period, we will import under legally questionable circumstances an attractive man or woman from a non-English speaking country for your pre-scheduled wedding day.

*

Bob Marley Scholarship – Hey, star, if you shot the sheriff and did not shoot the deputy, this scholarship is for you. Since we don't believe in the accumulation of material goods in this transient world, mon, we just pass along a shitton of sweet, sweet ganja and hope that it helps you on your educational journey. Rock on and do your ting.

*

Patriot's Scholarship – God Bless America. God bless Smith & Wesson.

Do you agree? If so, you may qualify for this scholarship. Please write a 10,000 word legal brief and press conference script on how to defend lax gun-ownership laws in this beautiful, courageous country, despite the, like, couple of gun-related deaths that the liberal media blows up each year. If you win, your brief may even be used by our legal team, once we hire replacements for the entire staff that quit after the latest "incident"! Hell, if you win, you may even be our legal team! Who needs college when you have guns, am I right? (This has NOT been paid for by the NRA. Seriously, guys why would you think that?)

*

Soulja Boy Memorial Fund – This is a scholarship for any fan that (1) remembers that rapper DeAndre Cortez Way (Soulja Boy) exists, (2) can name one song aside from "Crank That (Soulja Boy)" and "Kiss Me Thru the Phone," (3) has any interest at all in being associated with a scholarship named after Soulja Boy (DeAndre Cortez Way).

Honorable mentions:

❖ Children of Dictators Trust – Do you live in a dictatorship? Never met your dad, but know that you have 345 siblings? This trust is for you. Take it for the very slim possibility of making Daddy proud.

❖ Linux Users Fund – Know what a Linux is? Maybe you've used it? That's good enough for us!

❖ Optical Illusion Scholarship – Hey, check out these spiraling concentric circles! Wild, huh? Well, there's more where that came from! So why don't you keep on looking at that, and don't worry about college. If we keep the money, we can invest in cartels!

❖ Infomercial Scholarship – BUT WAIT! THERE'S MORE! IN ADDITION TO THE 7 SEMESTERS PROMISED, WE'LL THROW IN ONE MORE FOR A LIMITED TIME! IF YOU CALL NOW YOU CAN GET TWO FREE SEMESTERS FOR THE LOW PRICE OF JUST ONE HUG! JUST ONE! PLEASE!

11

Selected College Essays

You've gotten this far! Enjoy some practical examples of some excellent college essays, compiled though various crimes by the SatireV staff. We must leave you now, but if, against our wishes, you have chosen to apply to Harvard, best of luck.

✳ ✳ ✳

EXAMPLE 1: Reflect on a time when you challenged a belief or idea. What prompted you to act? Would you make the same decision again?

In elementary school, we were taught to treat people based on character, not on their skin color. Mrs. Koszczynski, my third grade health teacher, told us that black people, white people, "those damn Mexicans," Jews, and all other types of people are the same. Mrs. Koszczynski's talk of universal acceptance fundamentally revolutionized my worldview.

Eight years later, I was in the ninth grade. I was walking down the hall toward my locker after second period algebra, and I remember seeing a group of the "cool" kids pushing a Jewish kid around in the hallway. I recall becoming extraordinarily angry, to the point where my memory fails me when I think back to the next minute or two. Anyway, the next thing I remember is pushing all of the bullies aside and telling them that this poor lad had done nothing to them, and that they ought not to roughhouse him just on account of him being Jewish!

The group's leader shoved me back and said, "We're not pickin' on this kid 'cause he's Jewish. That's messed up, bro. We're pickin' on him 'cause he's gay as hell." I replied "well, in that case, I am deeply sorry," and I went on to third period.

As I continued down the hall, listening to the grunts and outcries of the gay kid behind me, I couldn't help but think to myself, "I did the right thing." Imagine if that guy hadn't been gay; I would have saved an innocent Jewish student from getting beaten up. Even before this event, I had prided myself on having a strong moral compass; this incident was no fluke.

I could go on, of course. There was the time I got upset because a Latino employee did not make as much money as a white employee in the same profession, but it turns out that the Latino employee was a woman. With each of these instances, though, I can guarantee that I would make the same decision again in a heartbeat.

There is nothing quite like the rush I feel when I do something right. Even though she was little more than a lowly Polish peasant, Mrs. Koszczynski certainly changed my life for the better. I can only hope that my actions encourage others to take the road less traveled and to stand up for what is right.

EXAMPLE 2: Supplementary Diversity Statement: Given your personal background, describe an experience that illustrates what you would bring to the diversity in a college community, or an encounter that demonstrated the importance of diversity to you.

From Harlem to Harvard
by Pennyworth Buckles

Since the beginning of time, man has wondered how best to live his life.

I am Pennyworth Buckles, and I am one of those men.

It all started on the Upper West Side of Manhattan, on the last day of junior year. After the last bell rang and my family tutor went home, I got ready for my early evening stroll. This time, however, I felt like doing something new, like I was confined by my surroundings. Perhaps it was the same smell of roses on the kitchen table. Perhaps it was the cold marble that tickled my toes after a rejuvenating shower. Perhaps it was the familiar wink that the bellhop gave me as I stepped through the lobby.

But I was ready for a new experience. That day, instead of walking through The Park, I would venture northeast—to an area where I was told there were "projects." Little did I know that these projects would be vastly different than the projects I had worked on for particle physics class at school.

As I walked, the streets' names became unfamiliar and the normal hum of high-rise central heating systems faded into the distance. I fancied myself an explorer in an uncharted territory. And soon I would have the pleasure of meeting the inhabitants.

Soon the buildings became decrepit, and had graffiti all over them. The streets became darker, as the sun descended. It was, to admit, a bit frightening. But I had to remember that I was an explorer after all: there was no reason to be afraid. It was just new territory.

Going down a side street, I walked into a local candy shop. The man behind the front desk greeted me. I can't exactly remember his name, but let's call him Jamal for now. I always liked that name.

Jamal said "Hello" and asked if there was anything in particular that I was looking for. Being in my explorative mood, I decided that I would, as some say, "free-form," and browse the shelves. The store offered an exhilarating selection of eateries completely foreign to my knowledge, with crude spellings I had never seen before—Laffy Taffy and Dum Dums. But the best name I saw I simply had to try: "Kit Kat."

I paid only 75 cents for the "Kit Kat." I commented to Jamal that the price seemed too low...that it may have been the price back in my grandfather's day, when his business acumen managed our trust fund's smaller sum before today's rapid inflation. His eyes danced in a rolling motion as he swiped my gold card in the machine.

I then walked back to my neighborhood, the Kit Kat in my hand, swinging through the streets of Manhattan. My visit had visibly changed me, I had more power, more swagger in my walk. I had seen a different part of the world, coming back different but stronger and better.

This moment in my life was meaningful not only for how it changed me, but also for making me realize the common humanity in us all. It's hard to leave one's shell, but when one travels outside of it, one realizes that one is among many ones, all of whom are similar in many ways. This lesson I would take with me to Africa in my gap year (see supplemental essay 1)—a place that reminds me of the Manhattan neighborhood I walked through that fateful day. And I would take it with me for the rest of my time in high school. And finally, I hope to take it with me to Brown this fall. I visited Harvard's campus last spring and have been dreaming in Crimson ever since.

So, going back to my original point, how does a man live the best life? That's simple: by living the one he wasn't meant to live, at least part of the time. One should always strive for new experiences, outside of one's norm. Otherwise, life would get very boring.

I hope to have many new experiences going forward with my life. And my greatest hope, one that has driven me to write to you today, is that my next new experience is at another unexplored territory for me—Cambridge. In other words, I hope Harvard can become my Harlem in the fall.

With grandest wishes,

Pennyworth Buckles

EXAMPLE 3: Some students have a background or story that is so central to their identity that they believe their application would be incomplete without it. If this sounds like you, then please share your story.

As John Steinbeck once said, "I've seen a look in dogs' eyes, a quickly vanishing look of amazed contempt, and I am convinced that basically dogs think humans are nuts." I, for one, have looked in the eyes of many a dog during my volunteer hours at the SPCA, and I believe that Mr. Steinbeck underestimates the canine brain. I believe that dogs see humans as humans. Maybe they sometimes confuse them with apes or orangutans, but they would almost certainly never perceive the human form as a nut. Pistachios are nuts. Almonds are nuts. Coconuts, however, are not nuts, and neither are people.

Apart from my time at the SPCA, where I had the privilege to nurse many a furry friend back to health in my arms, I have also gained valuable perspective into the psychological world of the dog through my interpretation of Snoopy in my high school's production of *You're a*

Good Man, Charlie Brown. During months of rehearsals, I found myself increasingly embodying the world of my character. For instance, I bought myself a doghouse to sleep in, and I would only eat and drink from bowls that my dutiful younger sister would place on the floor. Eventually, I even got fleas, and I started to shed. I didn't recognize my friends, and my coursework quickly fell by the wayside in my pursuit of the thespian ideal (this is the reason why all of my grades for the fall of my junior year are marked as "incomplete" on my transcript). I forgot who I was, and all I knew was Snoopy. I let myself be taken over completely by the shadow of the anthropomorphic pet. It was a wonderful experience.

On opening night, I sang my songs impeccably, and peppered my monologues with whimsically improvised barks, yowls, and whimpers. My drama teacher told me afterward that my performance was reminiscent of David Bowie's seminal portrayal of Jareth, the Goblin King, in the classic 1986 film *Labyrinth*. Needless to say, I was greatly honored by the compliment, and at Harvard, I would be sure to contribute to any number of dramatic productions, whether as the protagonist or as the quirky supporting character who steals the show with his wit and charm.

Unfortunately, the run of *You're a Good Man, Charlie Brown* had to be cut short, because apparently both our Linus and our Lucy were allergic to dogs, and my portrayal caused them to suffer severe congestion that ruined their singing voices and caused extremely painful headaches that prevented them from looking into spotlights for several weeks. Dozens of tearful theater-goers received refunds for their tickets, despite their pleas that the production merely be postponed. As a dutiful thespian myself, I cannot say that I agree with the school administration on this point. As Freddie Mercury wisely sings in Queen's hit "The Show Must Go On," "the show must go on."

EXAMPLE 4: Discuss an accomplishment or event, formal or informal, that marked your transition from childhood to adulthood within your culture, community, or family.

Most adults can look back and point to a single moment in their lives that shaped their path forever. Whether it's the first time they solved a calculus problem, driving them into the world of engineering, or the first time they skimmed $40,000 from a school fundraiser and recognized their passion for tax law. For me, it was the day I met Secretary of State John Kerry.

It all started back in April of 2013, when I realized I hadn't done anything remotely interesting enough to write a college essay about. Panicked, I sent applications to a variety of volunteer programs, summer abroad institutes, and pharmaceutical trials seeking human test subjects. To round out my options, I also sent e-mails threatening to overthrow the dictatorial governments of North Korea, Laos, Angola, and Sweden. After receiving a number of disappointing responses, including a rejection from a trial of Pfizer's new diabetes vaccine and a pension check from the Swedish government, I received a text-alert notifying me that the Republic of Angola had just declared me an enemy of the state. I called up my buddy who has a contact that provides fake IDs to kids at my high school, got a fake passport made and, within a few weeks, was on a flight to Luanda.

On the last leg of my journey, I learned something about myself: I'm a huge coward. Minutes after arriving in Luanda, a customs agent noticed my fake passport, recognized my face as belonging to a wanted man, and called security. Before the AK-47-armed transit police could mobilize, I bolted, running out of 4 de Fevereiro Airport and into the city streets, where I managed to elude capture for the hours it took me to reach the outskirts of the city. From there, I used my marathon training to run the 22 miles to the banks of the Cuanza River and the relative safety of Quicama National Park. I was quickly adopted by a small herd of reintroduced elephants, and I used my Boy Scout skills and experience working at a veterinary clinic to survive and ingratiate myself among the herd. Unfortunately, I underestimated the ruthlessness of the runt of the herd, Sambo, who betrayed me to the park rangers in exchange for 12 peanuts and a banana after three weeks of hiding.

The detention center I was brought to was atrocious; bread and water were the only sustenance, mosquitoes bred freely, and only the shiv-making skills I acquired while teaching physics through my church's prison ministry kept me from becoming a victim of the other hardened criminals housed within. After three weeks, satisfied that my experiences were sufficiently meaningful to fill a college essay, I reached out to my father's contacts in the State Department. Secretary Kerry, eager for a win after the international fallout from the Snowden leak, came to Angola personally to negotiate a prisoner exchange.

Seeing the elder statesman in person, deftly making his case and convincing the Angolan government to trade me for a Miami-imprisoned Cuban man wanted for war crimes during the Cuban intervention in the Angolan Civil War, I realized exactly what I wanted to do with my life. From that day forward, I dedicated myself to marrying into a condiment empire and using the money to finance a failed bid for the presidency. Harvard, which serves as a magnet for young heiresses, is the perfect place to make my dream come true.

About the Author

Founded by Ari Simon and Ari Weisbard in 1998 in Wigglesworth Hall, Satire V is Harvard College's student-run satirical newspaper, providing commentary on political, social and Harvard-specific events. Along with extensive online content, Satire V publishes a print edition every semester and produces comedic films and short parodies throughout the year. Satire V's alumni include *Bob's Burgers'* Dan Mintz, along with many other illustrious writers and comedians like William Shakespeare and Kathleen Sebelius. Visit us at: www.satirev.org

About the Illustrator

The Crunch Magazine, founded in October 2012, is the only student-run organization at Harvard College dedicated to promoting awareness and appreciation of sequential art. Each semester they produce a publication called *The Crunch* that features student-made artwork of all styles, topics and genres. *The Crunch*'s goal is to put forth a professional, funky, educative, magazine that help readers appreciate comics as an artistic medium. Visit us at: www.harvardcomics.com

Writers

William Keith
James Garcia Alver
Karen Chee
Matthew Disler
Shaan Erickson
Mercedes Flowers
Jackson Gzehoviak
Tyler Jankauskas
Ben Martin
Andrew Medina
Fola Sofela
Jonathan Young
Dashiell Young-Saver

Artists

Cover Art by Faye Zhang (Chapters 9 & 10) and Caroline Juang
(Chapters 2 & 7)
Ben Adegbite (Chapter 6)
Laila Carter (Chapters 3 & 5)
Daire Gaj (Chapter 1)
Jessica Jin (Chapters 4 & 8)